The Sym

CW00503929

Al;o by Michele Fermanis-Winward
and published by Ginninderra Press

Threading Raindrops
The Eucalypt Distillery
A Larrikin in the Blood
These Weighted Months
To the Dam (Pocket Poets)
The Sail Weaver (Pocket Poets)
Curdled Milk (Pocket Poets)

Michele Fermanis-Winward

The Symbiotic Web

Acknowledgements

Some versions of poems have appeared previously in *Mountain Secrets* anthology, *The Crow* journal and *Add To Cart* magazine.

Continuing gratitude is due to my fellow poet and editor, Brendan Doyle. I offer loving thanks to critic, spell check and geology tutor, my husband Kevin, whose love and support makes this collection possible. These poems were edited with the assistance of a Varuna Writer's Space Fellowship.

I live and work on the unceded lands of the Darug and Gundungurra people. I pay my respects to these traditional owners and to elders past and present.

I dedicate this collection to Mother Earth

The Symbiotic Web
ISBN 978 1 76109 355 5
Copyright © text Michele Fermanis-Winward 2022
Cover image: Mother Goddess Figurine, Old Babylon,
pre-1600 BC, Archaeology Museum, Istanbul

First published 2022 by
GINNINDERRA PRESS
PO Box 3461 Port Adelaide 5015
www.ginninderrapress.com.au

Contents

Introduction

Much has been written on connectedness, the human need to be part of something greater, our yearning to belong to one another, to bear witness and be witnessed, to assuage the great singularity, to know our spark of life was observed.

As a visual artist, I am driven to record my experience, to gather ephemeral and discarded objects I find, be they rusted tools or perfect but fragile shells of seed and pod, as objects to be revered. I am inspired by the diversity of nature, watching the details in the small world around me, the patterns of growth and decay.

I retreat, decline the temptations of society, the noise outside, proud to call myself a recluse. I am keenly aware that my time is closing in and am eager to finish the projects at hand. I will raise my voice against injustice and cruelty to others in the world – it is a sacred duty – while acknowledging that I am pampered and privileged.

For me, a poem starts with a line or phrase, a thought that stirs me, inspired by some thing I have seen or heard or thought. Then words appear on the page, they generate the next line, the next thought, as rhythm and form take shape. Then over time, this story I have made, be it a meditation, celebration or a protest, is worked over like a lump of rock, rough edges are polished, the grit removed. What am I trying to say, does it make sense, does it flow, are there better ways of saying it? Until I feel no more can be done.

My words bring together a life of image making, knowing the world I observe is disappearing because of climate change. We are all connected – like trees, our web spreads wide. The cheap dress I wear is made possible through another woman's poverty. My easy flick of a light switch contributes to the loss of habitat elsewhere.

This collection of poems draws on my deep love of the natural world. I decry its abuse and the rejection of first nations' wisdom. We belong to nature, she does not belong to us. She is our mother, to be loved and respected unconditionally.

Time Traveller

Between the grind
and clunk of city trams
glare from light and glass
I hear a disembodied cry.

Above my head a solitary crow
winds round our trees of steel
calling for its mate
and I am back in Mungo land.

There the silence of its dunes
was broken by a flint-voiced crow
a sound to slice millennia with
as the bird strutted in my shade.

Crows saw us humans come
new songlines scrolled
through red earth and blood
followed in our footfall tracks.

They watched us spread
dodged our spears and guns
as we cleared their feeding grounds
they prospered on our fallen stock.

Crows claimed this land
despite the laws to hunt them out
they bind us to the wild untamed
the ancient heart of us.

Returning to the Nest

Paddocks decked with fresh-rolled hay
to feed the herds and flocks
insurance for hard summer months
of parched bare earth forecast.

Above our heads a watercolour sky
dry brushed and washed
roadside grasses reaching for the sun
are billowing with seed.

Nothing here has changed
birds teach young to fly
to navigate by tree and watercourse
the angle of landmark to wing.

Like them we soar again
the seeming endless road
carries us back home
to ease the longing in our hearts.

The Outsider

I enter the garden
by its tree-shrouded gate
vines and weeds block my way
stems are interwoven
or hang limp, broken by the rain.

Thistle heads powder in the breeze
daisies tumble over stones
and rose canes arabesque
to catch unguarded skin
while snails add weight to every leaf.

What had been my heart's familiar
when I left it winter bare
with half a year of absence
my paths and beds so overgrown
now they greet me as a stranger.

Softly in the World

How grateful I am
to wake each day wrapped in clouds
to be here on our low mountains
of fretted escarpments.

Perched on a wooded ridge
with the valley far below
where wombats and wild dogs
spend lives untouched by man.

Parrots enter my garden
they bring me offerings of wonder
trees whisper to their young
pass on the ritual of growth.

I have learnt to heed
the push and pull of seasons
my own decay and loss
to accept the benediction of age.

Lichen

Life form with days unhurried
a symbiote of many colours
from desert heat to mountain heights.

Clinging by the shores of oceans
vibrant orange face-painted cliffs
and furry efflorescence.

Forest shrouds bathed in mist
conjure ghosts and witch's bowers
of being trapped by their green fingers.

Paddocks flecked with granite boulders
where colonies of algae bloom
married to their fungi.

Like handmade lace that's slowly wrought
it feeds on light and welcomes rain
while capturing our carbon.

Sensitive

The raucous cries of wattlebirds
hammer blows on soft grey sky
a blousy wind above my head
winnowing dry leaves
behind it all
a whir of traffic on the ridge.

Silver trunks
of fresh-peeled mountain ash
glowing in the sun
long strands of bark
looping through the bush
on tender ferns and wattle buds
ripening to burst.

The fragile interplay
of us and wilderness
our taming bush with tracks
to find a breathing space
here I can slough the mask
worn as my defence
against our noise and busyness
be free as any raw skinned tree.

Interface

A morning walk along an edge of scrub
the distant snarl of chainsaws slicing wood
deep forest gums are felled
and new homes rise from concrete pads.

Mint bush and honey notes combine
no tracks of foot or paw are seen
I am the first along this path
scrubbed smooth from heavy rain.

A spinebill pipes and another
in response across the waking ridge
I disturb a fledgling parrot
its urgent dash and squawk, too-fast wingbeat
then crash on mountain devil spikes.

The scene resumes its ordinary sounds
a whipbird calls above the insect drone
magpie twins watch, unsure if I'm a threat
behind it all the grunt of tractors clearing scrub.

Realigned

They hunker down, dun-coloured project homes
look up at rough-barked trees
with turf rolled out it's back to work and school
the hammering of men replaced by vacant glass.

In fresh turned earth native grasses seed
a thread of vine holds sapling gums unseen
one stem in leaf becomes a thatch of scrub
its dense untidy edge aligns new boundaries.

Undisturbed, lizards bask on rocks
draw in birds and snakes, the balance reaffirmed.

Intruders

Mountain ash and ferntree fronds
the gully falls to my right
lichen-soft wattle trunks quenched by mist
the scent of growth an interplay of rain and sun.

Mountain devils shoot red sparks
ignite dull shades of green
each blade and leaf evolved to mountain side
the vagaries of climate's many twists.

On season's cusp, nuances of changing light
pores open, close and wait for warmth
random shafts of pine are interlopers here
birds feast on aromatic cones.

Radiatas dwarf escarpment homes
on the streets, old windbreaks lining farms
great hulks but frail, crashing in high storms
fierce candles stoking fires.

Their seeds entice black cockatoos,
ranging tree to tree on loping wings
marked by piercing cries
heralds of the trees they spread.

A pine nut drops into an envelope of sand
the winnowed wash a breaking down of cliffs
it sets, survives, matures and falls
creates a home for other lives to bloom.

Black Cockatoos

Beneath the soft-lipped clouds
we scan a range of trees
hard forests still provide
cones with seeds and nuts.

This ridge of pines
is our favourite hunting ground
but people and their dogs
we keep clear distance from.

Our chick has fledged
he seeks wood grubs
and works beside us now
beaks out the fatty lumps.

When cold flows in
some foods grow scarce
turn thin and parched
then we must journey north.

Join the chorus of our flock
slow beat into the warmth
here plump casuarina stands
restore our strength to nest.

The Raiders

With strands of pliant ivy
round and round I work
creating nests for apples
to hang in my bare trees.

Late winter treat for possums
no leaves, they feed on bark
gnaw my rhubarb to the earth
strip lemons, mandarins.

Five baskets left overnight
tomorrow I'll add hooks
hang them through my garden
with offerings of fruit.

Secretly
my work is closely watched
pairs of robbers wait
in fading light they strike.

Now baskets lodge unseen
in shrubs and forks of trees
to line with feather quilts
for eggs of bandit birds.

This Shy Bird

Each day I hear you calling
rarely seen in urban gardens
your deep grey plumage
and wary eye ready for alarm.

Your distinctive call
higher pitched with double notes
than more familiar currawongs
who lilt and swoop
prising snails from rocks.

We feared for smaller birds
then heard among the shrubs
high pipes and chattering
they ignore your presence here
as each will claim their space
without concern from us.

Waking to Their Song

Through glass and brick
to my soft quilt of sleep
a bird is calling me to rise
the morning opening
its petals of light.

No buds are seen today
this drought makes barren ground
once perfumed air
floated out from thorny stems
to halt a passer-by.

Still birds have come
from small brown chirps
to magpies with their swirling trills
my garden blooms
in many flowers of song.

Winter Robins

They stand on guard
rosy pink or yellow breast
males watch and wait
for my turning spade
fat grubs exposed to light.

Around them bushes shiver
a host of dun-grey females
forage in the leaves
flitter, dive for insects
chatter all the time.

I do not hear their signal
a cloud of wings
whirls past my ears
leaves me with their echo
still brightening the day.

Simple Pleasures

I am soothed by isolation
the distractions of noise
that feed our world today
are muted in my sanctuary.

Still the heart grieves
how could it not
when so much loss exists
and forecasts more tomorrow.

Despair comes to many
the grim shadow we push aside
when lives are filled with action
finds us as sorrow's children.

In the turning of a patch of soil
the planting out of herbs and weeds
I am given this meditation
on giving and receiving life.

Skyscaping

While we sleep
snuggled under quilts
possums dance
across the branches far above.

Bending to their weight
leaves now brush the ground
and bounce
become trapeze for nocturnal feats.

Their alleyways are newly made
some retain this altered shape
and come the light
we find a branch now blocks our path.

We lop or tie them back
to save our heads from harm
then through the night another route
is weighed and bending down.

Synaesthesia

My eyes decode the colour blends
of bush in miniature from overview
a hum of saturated visual sound
within the forest's layered tones.

The terracottas of new leaves
crimson, mauve and yellow flowers
bark textures – beetle-pocked or
stripped to shed, thigh smooth
beneath their rough discarded shells.

A labyrinth of insect traps
spiders' webs strung through trees
crosshatch my skin as I pass.
My buzzing gnat of sight
is snared in silken threads of art.

Attraction

I gaze entranced at spiders' webs
their innate skill to span a gap
launch silk to sail the breeze
and forge complex geometry.

The punctuation marks on my walks
of patterned gum bark after rain
and twisted knots of drifted wood
each beauty wrought by chance.

I hoard pottery shards, shells and stones
see value in a nest of rusted wire
corroded and abandoned scraps
displayed to be admired.

I gravitate to things small
ephemeral and quirky asymmetrical
collections grow with the years
mementos of my time on earth.

Syncopation

Memory is fluid
what we recall
is a string to pluck
and when it resonates
we add it to our song.

The throb of longing
for all that's passed
once we were loved
old dreams recalled
to exaggerate and cull.

We can build a concert
from these old refrains
in the tempo of regret
or create an impromptu
disregarding all the rules.

For Love

Somewhere in the dark
a frog is calling for its mate
the earth is opening to rain
beneath a haloed moon.

This dull brown life
dormant underground
sensed a familiar chill
surround its sleeping form.

Soft mud against the skin
wakes his beating heart
slipping, struggling, sliding back
digging upwards to the light.

Pushing past the ooze
until he bathes in air
the scent of water
pulsing though his veins.

Searching for a pool
one no other claims
resounding through the night
his constant clunking need.

Deep Listening

I step outside
am bathed in song
alarms and welcome
from birds both large and small
white cockatoos, king parrots and rosellas crowd
a wattlebird's sharp response atop its banksia cone
spinebills pipe from fuchsia scrub
the magpie at my feet scrolls notes to draw his mate
I scatter seed for them.

The day opens into winter sun
abundant for this time of year
wind softens to a breath
the noise of man cannot be heard
I sit and listen to the land
feel its pull as any creature would
the scent of growth and decay
coursing through my skin.

I am a single shoot
connected to earth time
it does not count in years but seasons fat or thin
my bounty is not size but lives who nurture me
and those I feed in return
my body is a twig
to bend and grow
or break and start again
be part of the great web.

Respite

I gaze through trees
up to blue skies, no smoke
or wind or threat of fire
this vignette of a perfect day.

A frog calls from the pond
here the soil lies deep
it's sheltered by tall gums
the cost of recent storms unseen.

A flock of gang gangs land
squawking in the yard out back
their native habitat is gone
no food to give their young.

The bush beyond my fence
soil burnt, no seeds to crack
they forego a natural fear
will risk my dog and beg.

Among Friends

They show us how to live
generously
they are not possessed
by mal-intent
their one desire
to be the best they can.

Fed by light and rain
they give so much
to creatures everywhere
from roots to trunk and branches
in leaf or fruit and flower
we are surrounded by their grace.

They teach us how to share
this wondrous gift of life.

The Eucalypts

Round-headed trees lining childhood streets
hot days transform them to red balls of noise
parrots gorging on their flowers.

Widow makers spreading tall and wide
winds swirl, snap gangly limbs, unheralded
they fall as men work underneath.

Mallies contort, speak of hard times
dirt poor and tough, dry retching in the heat
a curse on soldier-settler claims.

Leafless sentinels from the ringbark days
cast adrift they pockmark rolling paddocks
between eroded creeks.

Ghost gums, icons of our desert heart
bound in dry river beds and shifting sand
white trunked galleons in full sail.

Mountain ash climbing for the sun
tall and straight stripped to truncated poles
leashed by wires they keep our streets alight.

I've seen them pruned, shrub-sized in Italy
as leaf-littered shade on parched Greek isles
but always best when free to spread at home.

The Sentinels

There are giants above us
hardwood with fissured bark
dull grey of limb and trunk
they twist towards the sun
overlap and groan as they rub
bow and flex in the wind.

Once deeply forested on the ridge
these gums die slowly one by one
dense understorey fades to grass
decay comes from the edges in
prey to disease and chainsaw men
the canopy grows sparse.

When the land is bare of trees
and storms come charging up the cliffs
we will find ourselves exposed
no shelter from the guardians
who protected all our years
we will be felled like them.

Banksia Serrata

I've loved this tree
for twenty years
planted as a five-leafed twig
with roots of tender filaments.

Through these years
of drought and storm
winds that tore others down
she endured and grew.

Tall among surrounding trees
with knobbly trunk
and gangly limbs
setting fruit to tempt the birds.

Black cockatoos
would bring their young
an easy perch for new-found wings
to feast upon her cones.

Now she is parched
down to the deepest root
must sacrifice her weakest limbs
their leaves turn brown and fall.
I pray she lives to fruit again.

The Lost Garden

As another of my rhododendrons dies
from lack of water
and hot soil binds its shallow roots
I consider the twenty years
of patient tending with hose and bucket
to make a sanctuary called home.

Today dust rises as I rake the paths
a taint of smoke is in the air
and I wonder what another year
will bring this patch of ground
that love, manure and compost
could not protect from drought.

Disreputable

Like dissolute old men
Radiata pines
hang out in parks
form tight-knit groups.

Some lean in
as if to hear tall tales
from blokes who'd know
share jokes.

All gap toothed, worn bark
and threadbare limbs
of hard times living rough
prefer a drink to food.

Look down on youngsters
shooting for the sun
trust a hollow worn by time
and mates who have their backs.

Sasanquas

As the season takes on
its autumnal tones
they enter the limelight
pink and white and blousy
on high-sprung stems
exotic dancers in display.

Like a stage door Johnnie
the wattlebird strikes
feasts on their nectar
scatters petals like coins
squawks at his rivals
guards these cold-day girls.

The Divas

After the fires
the charring of my ground
roses are blooming again
they crowd this autumn yard.

Now bare-stemmed
I grieve the loss of some
those stars of summers past
brought life to languid days.

I will no longer see
their opening to warmth
dressed in satin gowns
swirling perfume on the wind

New buds are dancing now
this sunshine is for them
blending scented melodies
and learning how to sing.

Bearding the Iris

It comes from errant seed
lodged beneath the lemon's shade
each year leaves multiply
give one bloom to summer warmth.

Above long straps of green
through tangled citrus stems
I catch a glimpse
of something taupe and strange.

Like any supplicant
on hands and knees
avoiding thorns above my head
I come into its lair.

Delicate as a butterfly
with exotic insect form
the intricate patterning
of stippled throat and fluted tongue.

It gives no shout of perfume notes
no gaudy shade to attract
here soft tones of gold and fawn
wait out of sight for one discerning bee.

Wild Roses

They have been set free
from their allotted garden beds

No longer bound
in nurserymen's strict aisles
the plant breeders of conformity
to colour, size and perfume.

From parents with neat labels
their offspring ramble
swing from branches, wander laneways
like children out of school.

They have no interest in another's history
they want to make their own
sweetening the air
with a scent of vanilla and honey.

Ready to snare a passer-by
with innocent simplicity.

Banksia Rose

The air electrifies
now the sky darkens
gathering shades of ash
slender branches contort
heavy with flower.

Thunder ripples
billows from rain squalls
wind tugs at new leaves
filled with sap
and strengthened by the test.

The yellow rose trembles
then settles back
to weave new canes
among the trees
buds open and quenched.

Once held by iron
now rusted, bent with age
stems push through
seeking new support
outward to the light.

Survivor of hard prunings
no transient storm
will stop its primal urge
obedient to one law
to grow and grow and grow.

Reading Water

Trees ooze carmine sap
it hardens on wet bark
soft green a downy lichen
shelters in the fog.

Small shards from pots
washed by days of rain
reveal the printer's art
of a hundred years ago
oxide patterns gleam
against the burnt red earth.

Above my head two magpies
teach song to speckled young
the fluid notes are tumbling
like marbles over rocks.

My brother phones
he's one day north by car
and bathed in tropic sweat
I hear the sound of boys
who laugh and splash
beside him in the pool.

Between us farms in flood
a remnant of this storm
turns me back to close
the pages of my day.

On This Wet Day

Here in the mountains
waratahs light red beacons
through the bush and banksias
are bursting with new growth.

Up north fires are raging
whole towns are threatened
with being swept from maps
despair marks a local's face.

The farmer sees his life's work
his kid's future turn to ash.
How I wish that it could rain
somewhere else today.

Quenched

Outside
the world looks small
mist encloses all I see
is colour-washed
to grey and black
the thatch of branches
water dulled
and lichen couched.

A solitary car
passes down the lane
accompanied by
an unfamiliar sound
tyres splashing
through the rain
to slake my thirsty heart.

The Rampage

An angry wind rummages through the yard
whips young growth on drought hardened trees
soft grounded plants cannot resist
exposure of their roots
those delicate tendrils thirsting for rain
like hatchlings with mouths always open.

Respite is momentary
an inhaled breath before the next blow
nerves stretched by hours of worry
we fall to restless sleep
as the night placates a furious sky
and masks the daylight's shambles.

Beaten Back

Today the wind
forces me inside
a sunhat impossible to wear
snagged by rose thorns
grasping from a branch above.

My eyes are grit-balls
become dry slits of pain
dirt blown up my nose
could host an insect colony.

At night in bed
the house encased in noise
branches hold a voodoo beat
eclipse the possum's race
buffeting our roof.

Our bin wobbles down the lane
its drunken dance
ending in collapse, the rubbish
swirls wanton in display.

Sheltering

The bureau forecasts snow
leaves no longer tremble
they lash a soft grey sky
twigs shed like heavy rain.

As treetops crash together
against the weight of clouds
eucalypts' blue shadows
cast twilight into rooms.

Red maple leaves break free
they dart among the bushes
like startled wrens
seeking cover from the storm.

Folding In

Beyond the glass
there is only absence
wind no longer beats against the house
birds are gone or quietly dozing.

The last leaves hang listless
waiting their turn to fall
as golden tones fade to brown
my view becomes a palisade of twigs.

It is the closing in of winter
when the world outside these rooms
and the one that's here inside
are most divided.

My contact with the earth
a knowledge of the shape
and need of every plant
is fading while they sleep.

Come spring I will go out
delight in each new growth
my blood rising like sap
as we burst to life again.

Compromise

Contained
like roses in their planter pots
they wrapped a square of land
around themselves
maintained the rituals
that expressed their love
doted on wild birds they fed.

Their dogs were treated as
more human than was kind
the bitch and male tried to be
childlike where they could
were scolded when
the canine urge broke free.

The problem was resolved
as the couple learnt
to be more like their dogs.

Dry Winter

I'm tucked in bed
by coffee, dog and husband warmed
outside a spinebill pipes
clear notes dissolving in grey mist
clouds lift, reveal transparent blue.

We are restricted by the law
and our enduring drought
thus my garden thirsts
plants show signs they soon will fade
will not survive the test.

Earthworms no longer seen
the ground hard pressed
or soft as dust falling from my hand
strong winds could blow away
unless more stones are laid.

There are signs outside of animals unseen
holes dug to plunder roots
they chew dead wood
as birds gather in the trees
wait for me to give them seed today.

When Our World Was White

I recall winters in the snow
when the sky turned ashen tones of green
I watched the flakes
slip through vacant trees, swirl and melt
before they touched the ground.

Sometimes it snowed all night
the garden bound beneath its silent weight
soft mounds of shrubs and pots
draped porch and washing line
clothes hung like rigid ghosts.

Today this story of the past
seems as a painted fairy tale
like wolves and riding hoods
my midwinter gloves and heavy coat
remain untouched again this year.

Backburn

At dusk
smoke insinuates through cracks
by windowsill and door
clings to curtains, clothes and skin.

Somewhere near
as our escarpment ridge
the bushfire threat is tamed
its undergrowth reduced to ash.

Creatures of the night
the native rat and mouse
emerging to a world turned black
to silent cat and fox exposed.

Seasonal Retreat

The leaves turned red
and then the wind
blew them into hollows
round the house.

We wake in icy chill
snuggle, stay in bed
until the heater purrs
thaws our lifeless rooms.

I shuffle papers, clothes and food
turn on the oven, bake
find ways to be enclosed
inside a cube of warmth.

The garden left to sleep
unattended by my steps
plans to mulch abandoned
mounds left to decompose.

The dog is getting plump
gives me her mournful stare
when I suggest a walk
she curls into a ball.

We're planning our escape
to a north coast beach
so I don another layer
while packing summer shorts.

I long for the ocean's serenade
and sunblocked walks
as my sandy dog and I
dance in and out of waves.

What Can We Hear

Beyond the road and car
a windmill creaks
and tin sheds hum with flies.

Long paddocks drone
ruled by the sun and bees
hills fatten into song.

We heard the requiem of drought
when all our lives reduced
marked time in prayers for rain.

We can slip the hours
find ourselves absorbed
in the music of this land.

Wind and rain are strings
to give a tree its voice
down to the smallest leaf.

A distant growl, white-vapour-trailed
long-haul flights made small
beneath the chant of birds.

The Wollar Road

Kangaroos skid across our path
in unfamiliar rain, lush grass appears
beneath fire blackened trees.

A home of wood and tin
had stood one hundred years
its memories now ash, washing to the dam.

Skeletons crowd the hills
no tree unmarked by flame
rock shelves exposed, eroding in the wet.

Here lichen covered cliffs
crack into mammoth blocks
and fresh-bared tracks are corrugating mud.

Causeways under water
where drought had ruled for years
roadkill skin and bone is flushed upon the tar.

Lightning ripples through the trees
safe within our Faraday cage
past thunderclaps and escarpment falls.

Sodden farms, weed strung fencelines
with muddy lambs shivering under trees
and ducks find refuge on the bridge.

After the Rain

New England hills
are sparsely wooded
like derro's stubble
in dieback brown and grey.

The road's a gleaming mirror
above us feldspar glints
caught by the sun
on granite boulder heights.

Fields of glowing buttercups
and Salvation Jane
the long paddock
is now a wildflower meadow.

We round a bend to change
here ochre termite nests
crowd the wastes
of vibrant purple weed.

Trestle bridges sag and buckle
the land grown hard
hosts straggly wattle scrub
and prickly pear abounds.

B doubles grinding on
to meet deadlines
are stopped mid-flight
as an echidna slowly waddles
past their steaming wheels.

Drowning in the Dark

He woke and felt the wet
oozing through his sheets
was this how death would feel
its chill creeping up his skin
like spider legs of ice
cold with fear he tumbled out of bed.

The pain of something hard and sharp
rippled through his leg
panic charging him awake
his heart revved like a two-stroke pump
at 96, frail and confused
in water to his knees.

Inside the van
possessions drowned or floating
blocked its narrow door
a flood was beyond his mind.
Some bastard did this to his home
he cried and cursed to the night outside.

Cut and bruised he could not walk
believed his world had ended here
a familiar voice circling somewhere close
he dreamt a neighbour dragged him free
among the wrecks in hospital
adrift on a raft of yesterdays.

Community

To bear the combined weight
of our own suffering
as we hold another in their grief
this is our shared humanity
our raft through dangerous seas.

To laugh and sing, to cheer
show our support
or mourn a sudden loss
this ring of care holds us close
we know it's here that we belong.

To lift a stranger as a friend
and value their heart as our own
without the need to keep a score
but for our deep awareness
of the brevity of every life.

I Recall

Swimming as a child
our local beach was ochre yellow
we found anemones and starfish
and there were stingrays
in the shallows.

The sand was strewn with
jellyfish and shark egg cases
we would gather mussels
harvest periwinkles
for our lunchtime feast.

Now the beach hosts
microplastics, lost thongs
ring pulls and drinking straws
discarded bits and pieces
in many tones and hues.

Down stormwater drains
flowing to the sea
processed by the waves.
I wonder what the colour
of tomorrow's beach will be.

The News From Home

Antarctic blasts
bring snow and ice
mountain folk shiver in the cold
trees fall
alas a much loved woman dies.

The power lines are cut
no heating for electric homes
as wind speed soars
above one hundred Ks
its chill feels like minus twelve.

I phone a friend
she's huddled deep in bed
bemoans her trees are bared
camellia blooms
lie shredded on the ground.

I do not know
how my home and garden fare
imagination brews
a scene of devastation
until I'm there again.

Broken Promises

In October
they open from tight nubs
with a green to make hearts ache
for lands our forebears knew.

Leaves delicate as insect wings
transform bare stems
with promises of growth
for the cycle to renew.

Within a day
leaves turn brown and crisp
buds of roses form then wilt
or opened for an hour are spent.

The garden limp and parched
hard soil denying life
this new rite of spring
when October is a summer month.

Giving In

I live among the ironstone
where shallow roots must strive
here leaves of dead and dying trees
lie thick upon the ground.

With luck some will revive
but not the foreign breeds
magnolias and azaleas
cede to the water-wise.

Each day I search for growth
and hesitate to prune
I've lost the will to fight
summer breaks the heart of spring.

A Call to Action

This war comes by degrees
one hundred years ago
the warning was ignored
we had just won
a war to end all wars
'let us enjoy the peace'.

Today glaciers retreat
and creatures fall extinct
you say, 'not in our backyard
a little loss here and there
is not too great a price
for all that we desire'.

Do we forgo the latest car
and fruit we cannot grow
or lose our home to fire
and children in a flood.
Now all of us must fight
to save our life on earth.

Tremor

We are a breath into the wind
a mote of random dust
against the mountain range
less than a spark beside the sun.
We are a tear that drops
unnoticed in the ocean swell.

No wonder that we rage
make believe with pomp and noise
we are masters of the world
lay waste to other lives.
But when earth shakes
we know how small we really are.

Sirens in the Night

Too young for fire drills
sixty years ago
sent home when fires threatened
eyes stinging from the smoke
not knowing if our classrooms
would survive the night.

We greeted summer
with sunburnt noses, salty skin
and the lick of fear
bushland ringed our streets
lush undergrowth held threats
of firebugs and snakes.

Parched days of north wind scouring
and super-heated grass
butts flicked from Holden windows
every adult smoked
a whiff of burning tea trees
sent us scrambling up the cliffs.

We marked fear in older faces
waiting on the beach
watched a thin white ribbon
diffuse an empty sky
spread and gather speed
flames darting at its base.

We remember the big ones
a home lost here or there
rates little mention in the news.
Roused by a pulse of sirens
we recall the scent of burning leaves
keeping us awake.

On Sharing

We complain in town
red dirt on glass and lungs
our washing streaked and stained
from someone else's land.

There a farmer and his wife
once fenced a patch of soil
the home paddock's fruit and veg
proud to have it thrive.

Then this long dry
they wept to see their cattle sold
no choice, the creek-fed dams
and bore had died.

Not much to show but debt
and miles of fine red dust
now it lifts into a roiling cloud
to land on someone else.

Relative Safety

Late January's furnace blast
of dry and flailing wind
she woke and feared the day
then watched as clear blue sky
shaped to clouds of smoke
their bases tinged with brown.

She tasted fire curling through the air
black leaves swirled about the yard
her breath grew thick
and she could barely see
now ember shots, red hot against her skin.

Forget the hose and in the car
with pets and chooks, no backward glance
too late to grab more than a mask and phone
escape the flames was all she asked
as they consumed her home.

Crowded in with friends and dogs
their refuge in the local hall
hugs and grief for all she lost
the garden and her years of work
no place for covid safety here
and she no longer cared.

Still Waiting

Through flood and fire or tempest
small towns confront their loss
the politicians come, mouth platitudes
the laying on of hands
tick them off a list and move on.

The town is left to grieve
waiting for relief, little comes
from all the pledges made
bogged down in building regulations
and few tradies on the ground.

In caravans and tents
the ones who chose to stay
watch their landscape
restored to vibrant green
while they wait to start again.

Forgotten

The fires came
and they survived
their cattle and their homes did not
now twelve months on
they feel abandoned by the state.

The pledge of aid is still to come
though all the forms were sent
fatigued by months of want
in tents and caravans
on land that needs their work.

Their dams are full and birds return
no pumps or lines
no tanks to hold the rain
the grass in paddocks grows
no stock will eat it down.

It moves as bright green waves
when summer turns the stalks to brown
and winds build to a furnace roar
the land will burn
and leave no trace of life.

We Can See You Now

With dogs and guns
on bloody spotlit nights
a bounty on their pelts
as vermin to our eyes
we strung them on the fence.

Ringbarked their homes by day
cursed wombat holes
and roos among our crops
blamed dingoes for dead lambs
clear-felled the land and sprayed.

So few of them remain
today their world is ash
with nowhere else to run
they look to us for help
trust that we have changed.

Paws clasped around a hand
we see them on our screens
their heads are turned
up to a human face
forgiveness in their eyes.

To Know This Day Alone

I walk the path where lilies bloom
and waratahs are setting seed
where cicadas thrum in trees
and bees drone round my head
step deep in spring's new growth.

Tomorrow's heat and summer winds
will silence all but urgent notes
I recall when flames eclipsed
mountain ash now shadowing the ridge.

Will peace remain in gullies far below
where possums doze and ferns expand unseen
or noise and swirling ash
turn every life to blind and boundless fear
in another fire's embrace.

Abiding

We are side by side
in early morning silence
holding the light and dark
of over thirty years together.

Through clouds of misunderstanding
the storms of disappointment and anger
we wake each day and renew our bond
knowing it abides in deep trust.

It is sure as any mountain
and deep as the gullies
that surround the home we made
for love in any weather.

Gratitude

Before a cloud envelops me
dissolves my thoughts to sludge
will I have time to tell the earth
I loved her all my days
the myriad variety
of wings and beating waves
of trees and mountain life
the sky above my hours?

Will I have one more chance
to clasp my friends
and tell them how their love
enriched my years
relieved the darkest night
will I have time enough
to know and still forgive myself
to find the grace I crave?

CPSIA information can be obtained
at www.ICGtesting.com
Printed in the USA
LVHW050627270722
724473LV00012B/427